What the Critics Have Said About:
A Tremendous Canada of Light

"Exciting, demanding, and pathbreaking… a bold
new answer to questions about Canada."
–Pierre Elliott Trudeau

"A new vision of Canada, freed of borders and race."
–John Ralston Saul

"Powe has discovered the roots of an informal
Canadian democracy and shows us its
poetry and wonder."
–Duncan Cameron, *The Toronto Star*

"Mr. Powe opens up avenues of thought and
feeling…. He offers a vision of Canada that is
positive and based on shared values."
–Carole Corbeil, *The Globe and Mail*

"B.W. Powe… presents a compelling case for Canada
as the world's first 'communication state'."
–Jean C. Monty, CEO, Northern Telecom, in the
Foreword to *The Canadian Internet Handbook*

"At a time when Canadian politicians are singularly
lacking in vision, Powe seems to have it in spades."
–Carol Rothman, *Montreal Gazette*

"An innovative view
–Brian Savage

A
CANADA
OF LIGHT

B.W. POWE

SOMERVILLE HOUSE
PAPERBACKS

Canadian Cataloguing in Publication Data

Powe, B. W. (Bruce W.), 1955-
    A Canada of Light

Previously published under title: A tremendous Canada of light
ISBN: 1-895897-89-0

1. Canada - Politics and government. 2. Canada - Civilization. 3.
Communication - Canada. I. Powe, B.W. (Bruce W.) 1955-   .
A tremendous Canada of light. II. Title.

FC630.P69 1997   971   C97-930069-X
F1034.2.P69 1997

Originally published in 1993 by Coach House Press, Toronto

Cover and text design: Tania Craan
Cover background photo: Ken Davis
Author photograph: Andrew Danson

Printed in Canada

Somerville House Paperbacks
Published by Somerville House Publishing,
a division of Somerville House Books Limited,
3080 Yonge Street, Suite 5000, Toronto, Ontario M4N 3N1
E-mail: sombooks@goodmedia.com
Internet: www.sombooks.com

Somerville House Publishing acknowledges the financial assistance of
the Ontario Publishing Centre, the Ontario Arts Council, the Ontario
Development Corporation, and the Department of Communications.

... and my eyes followed the spin of the fields newly laid out for sowing, the oak woods with hard bronze survivor leaves, and a world of great size beyond, or fair clouds and then of abstraction, a tremendous Canada of light.

Saul Bellow,
The Adventures of
Augie March

CONTENTS

THE ARGUMENT

The old Canada is ending. Nothing clear, fully voiced or formed has emerged in the raw, agitated state. Blurred lives, overwhelmed minds. So we start, moving out in all directions at once, thinking we have decades to make our choices, instead of years, or merely months, even days, or moments.

*

In the rampage of what seem to be terminal disagreements and divisions, rising confusions and intolerance, we can be certain only of this: our time and place have been electrified.

Electricity sparks, clings, looking for conductors and situations to illuminate, to jolt. Wherever energy cords crisscross, they bring new cords and discords–harmonies and alliances, turmoil and noise. Our amplifiers, which we call electronic technology, heighten the perpetual shifting which is life, making rampant change itself our exhilarating and harrowing circumstance.

Electricity alters our relationship with every social contract. Questions burst upon us: what is citizenship now? how do we remain individuals who can make choices and influence systems and institutions in the mass technological milieu? what is the role of government? who rules here? where are our borderlines? what are our responsibilities? how do we stay responsive—alive people not yet numbed, our souls not yet diminished or shrivelled by exposure to too much stuff, too many competing images and voices?

I am more and more moved by the question of what kind of state we will prefer when commerce and computers combine to launch and support a borderless economic world order. Must politics now be divorced from questions of the humane spirit, of justice in our lives? Are there alternative paths ahead?

*

Magnetism generates fields, electricity enhances flow. Electromagnetism melds field and flow in startling arrangements of attraction and repulsion.

One of these arrangements I call a Canada of light.

*

This light state is where history and time dance lightly. What I mean by this is the dancer's lightness of step, lightness opposed to heaviness or weight, opposed to tragedy and gloom, to traumatized and paralyzing experience. According to physicists, in Quantum Physics and Relativity, we are ourselves made of light and energy, we are beings who share in the particles and events of planets and moons, comets and stars.

I am referring here to a state of light-in-the soul, a lightness of spirit in a country that exists in contrast, striking contrast, to other societies.

The light state in Canada is where the wired world plays out one possible story, one myth I find exemplary for our anguished, wrangling world. We must learn how to breathe in this lightness—we must learn how to let it move us, lift us forward.

*

Pascal said, "Nothing stands still for us." Absolutes are delusions because we float on waves of possibly unknown extent and depth, we are vulnerable to winds and waves. Every fixed point will and must move. Yet we burn with the desire to find firm footing, lasting ground.

We have added to the old recognition that life is eternal turmoil. Global mayhem stuns us, rioting on an unprecedented scale, because our amplifiers, the electronic media, intensify consciousness, expand experience, and sear and shear our senses. Mass technologies hook us into the fundamental fields and currents of the universe; the wired and wireless machines accelerate and alter natural flux. We have created a machine-state that mirrors us, replicates us, renews us, and yet can alienate us from the world. In a terminal flash, electricity jumps up contraries, contradictions. William Blake's *The Marriage of Heaven and Hell* is an everyday occurrence; surrealism is the pulse of the streets. Ovid's *Metamorphoses* is now the stuff of reality, not fantasy; we are hurtled through Dante's *Divine Comedy* at night on our TVs, but without a Virgil to guide us, and without the promise of Beatrice's blessing at the end. The implicit contradictions in our minds and souls are rendered explicit at every turn by the electronic screening and exposure.

Cubism and pluralism are no longer an art movement and a political theory. They are facts, what we engage daily.

*

So we plug into electric currents and fields without first tuning ourselves, providing our psyches and sensibilities with insulation, the refinement of learning, self-knowledge. We rise and fall, crashing and cresting.

Out of tune we spin, but in tune we could dance.

*

Here is the etymology of the word, "electric". It comes from the Latin *electrum,* meaning amber, a fossil resin that exhibits electrical power when rubbed; and from a Greek root word, meaning a gleaming. Electricity occurs when energy poles between two objects of friction. That friction leads to sparks of light and to the paradox that light can be both a wave and a field.

And we need light to make our way.

*

This is Canada, the state I see: the flash-points of friction appear between Quebec and the rest of the country, between history and the always hazy present, between the old nation-state with its fixed borderlines and the new open state process, between the aboriginals' spiritual root-edness in the land and their trust in dialogue and the settlers' materialism and their demand for resolution, between desires for independence and originality and the need for channels between isolates, between evolutionary Canada and the revolutionary American empire. What do I mean by evolutionary? A culture and civilization in flux, in perpetual metamorphosis. What do I mean by revolutionary? A society defined or divided by revolution, insurrection, coup or civil war, conditioned by violence, bruised moods.

(A digression: the evolutionary model of Canada especially contrasts with the revolutionary model of America in the notion of solitude. In Canada it is still possible to be alone; in America there is a relentlessly public existence for everyone, with little quiet left for anyone.)

Quebec needs Canada because Quebec provides sparks of challenge, a current of passion, while Canada provides fields, larger contexts for the passion. One without the other would enfeeble the whole, leaving in pieces the traces of the grander latent scheme, the light state, fixed yet unfixed, a new kind of collage country, made of aboriginal dream songs and fierce polemics, private visions and media publicity, the first country to peacefully absorb the swing and shock that accompanies the electric infusion, the processing of fire.

*

Ancient philosophers were familiar with the elemental grounds of their times and places: earth, air, fire, water. I call fire, or energy, our true element.

The ancients were also familiar with a method they called poetic wisdom. Proofs lead to theory. My method is to make what I write an echo of everything I probe and read, and observe and absorb. What I've been proposing is not a theory, but a story about Canada that is also a poem and a fragment, a song and a broadside on the mysterious process occurring in a country that people struggle to define, or that people elsewhere overlook.

*

To arrive at a conclusion may be to arrive at the beginning: we may find that debate about who we are is what we are.

*

I'm drawn to this country's paradoxes and promises—the quiet passion and anomalies, the inward verve and subtle pulse of the magnetic north. Here discontinuities and abiding frictions appear to be necessary for our growth. Here I find a fascinating enigma, a conundrum of great beauty: Canada is a country that works well in practice, but just doesn't work out in theory.

*

We falter forward on an obscure path, we struggle to make guesses, we come to the questions of ruling and state, we envision a place where everything that is humane has not yet disappeared, we continue our search, because we sense a high form of civilization, of civility, is at stake. "Hurry slowly," the ancients said shrewdly. So it must be with us, now.

FIRST MEDITATION
In a Communication State

During his first Canadian winter, [Alexander Graham] Bell had resumed some of his former experiments with tuning forks…The harmonic, or multiple, telegraph [prototype of the telephone] was beginning to take shape. He spent hours in the little drawing room… singing a single note into the piano, his foot on the pedal, "listening for the answering vibration of corresponding key".

Avital Ronell, describing
Bell's thought processes, in
*The Telephone Book:
Technology-Schizophrenia-
Electric Speech-*

I perceive communication to be the value of Canada, the highest good of a state where understanding and misunderstanding, conciliatory conversation and vitriol, where constant negotiation and the limits of language, coexist. We have had to learn how to contact one another over an enormous land space, across five and a half time zones, in what was once a wilderness of scattered settlements, in what is now a sprawl of suburban edge cities and satellite towns. Technology forges connections and disconnections here.

Through the committees and meetings that first established the Canadian fact in 1867, through the language controversies and crises of unity, the public debates and referenda that have characterized Confederation, we can pick up, discern, this story developing: dynamic communication. The story carries a myriad of messages about the necessity of reaching one another, of patiently listening to each other, the urgency of continuous debate, the recognition that our individualized meaning must emerge from conferences, words, communiqués, images, signals, and vibrations sent over the air.

From the beginning, Canadians have had to lay railway track, build roads and bridges, dig canals, string wires from telegraph poles, set up telecommunication networks and centres and transmitters and receivers, establish the complex of links that will bind one coast to the other, make translations that conduct meaning from one language group to another, in an inextricable dialogue where resolution often seems remote, and unlikely. I take the CN Tower in Toronto to be a power point symbolic of invisible influx and transmission.Its motto: Welcome, Let Your Spirits Soar.

The reverse side of the hunger and need to communicate is the discharge of random chatter. This is the noise that can block out our better instincts, blank out the flow of sensitive, ethical consideration; this noise can be the grumbling and innuendo, the accusing and blaming, that retreats back into itself, into the political solipsism that we sometimes call regionalism. The communication fact makes our state a place and condition of multiple voices, not one voice, a polyphony that can become a deafening and stifling cacophony.

This restless communication field makes Canada perpetually difficult to define. Our history differs profoundly from that of the United States, with its individualist story, its militarism and commercialism, its violent conquests of space and people, its millenarian sense of Manifest Destiny. Creativity and cruelty collide in America. In Canada, people hug the borderlines between the provinces and the states, seek a community in cities and towns, construct vital links and support structures (railways, dams, hydroelectric projects, satellites), and then experience the inability to agree on what the country is about. Constitutional conferences and unity committees become a permanent process of breakdown and rebuilding. Yet many cultures and many often contradictory meanings breathe freely here. Vehement disagreements may mask or obscure the underlying faith that the process of confused and even acrimonious engagement, of stumbling incomprehension, those divisive showdowns that apparently sever goodwill from our experience, may be authentic, the path that leads to the sense of difference and respect which can reveal the harmony in our humanness.

We resist a final articulation of ourselves because we know, deep in our souls, that our story is about the process and value of communication itself. In this wide, spacious country, with its areas of privacy and calm, solitude and reverie can lift us and infuse us; here we may think, observe, comment, dream. Electronic intensities may deluge us, and they may be channelled. To communicate with others, with ourselves, with the landscape, through our machines, is our chief business; culture and the possibility of affinity and rapport, our primary hope; and talking and arguing, not to merely fill time, but to extend humane interplay beyond our provinces. We know that we have begun without a fixed idea of who we are and of where we are going. The tracks of communication, always shifting, are everything.

The story of Canada is one of the secret country, the place of inward people, contemplating and questioning the idea of nationhood, pondering what values we wish to see expressed and achieved. We wait, often perplexed, tempted by swirls of anger and hate, drawn to the barely spoken, to the dimming memories of what it took to make this ours, all the whisperings of a new world.

Remember:

The Confederation debates of 1864-1867.

Representatives from Canada West (Ontario), Canada East (Quebec), and the Maritimes, gathered in Charlottetown, Quebec City, and what was soon to be renamed Ottawa. They met and talked, and talked; and talked on, through the days, into the evenings. Earnest disputes and speechifying, argument and caucuses, bargaining and haggling, compromises and trade-offs. It was all "coaxing and wheedling", according to George Brown. The process was tentative, uncertain, slow, requiring time and patience. But the representatives negotiated to make a new transcontinental union. Sir John A. Macdonald affirmed that "this is the second time that man has founded a democracy in the new land..."

October, 1864, Quebec City.

By day, there were meetings, words, accommodations. At night, there were dinners, balls, informal conversations, dances.

Edward Whelan, a delegate from Prince Edward Island, said, "The Cabinet Ministers—the leading ones especially–are the most inveterate dancers I have ever seen; they do not seem to miss a dance the live-long night."

And south of the border?

By September 1864, the American Civil War had reached an apogee of bloody mania. Sherman had invaded Atlanta. In October, Confederate General Hood ambushed Sherman outside the city–though Hood's assault failed to stall Sherman's advance; at the same time, Union General Sheridan devastated the Shenandoah countryside. By November, Hood had retreated, and Sherman had razed Atlanta. Yankees swarmed to the sea, hunting rebels, destroying railways, looting mansions, torching crops, pillaging foodstores, until the South was humbled in 1865.

To the north, West Canadians, East Canadians, and Maritimers argued over unity. When they weren't debating unity, they were stating firm opinions over who should shoulder the better part of the national debt burden.

We must remember that the Canadian experiment was in part inspired by fear of the American Civil War and of the Fenian raids of the mid-1860s. Aware of the carnage to the south, alarmed by the efficient and restless military power of the victorious Union, Canadian politicians met to conceive of a different kind of state.

No one was coerced into signing the British North America Act. No individual or group was bullied, or hustled along by the barrel of a gun or by the sharp-edge of a bayonet during the debates. The words that the Fathers of Confederation set down did not dismay or incense any participating members from the three regions. English and Québécois politicians alike agreed out of self-interest and a strong sense of self-protection to make a state. The Québécois delegation—George-Étienne Cartier was one of its leaders—was promised that Quebec would have its own system within the larger system, a deliberate gesture that would preserve a measure of vital dissent inside the new country.

A symbolic or esoteric reading of the situation would reveal how Americans battled fellow Americans for their new unity, offering their lives, and that Canadians fought each other over the negotiating table, offering arguments, hesitations, compromises, and principles. When

Americans go mad and murderous, Canadians take notes and talk. Typically, the unity that the Canadians made was loose, provisional, varied, improvised. The document they produced, the BNA Act, was less definite and ringing than the American Declaration of Independence, or, for that matter, the French Declaration of the Rights of Man. The whole Canadian endeavour must have seemed quixotic, certainly paradoxical, in its yoking together of unlikely people, the French and the English, and those who settled the coasts and the interiors. *E Pluribus Unum* was achieved with war drums, flags, and shouts of a noble cause, over corpses and rubble. "Peace, Order, and Good Government" was achieved through mediation, speechifying, and agreements, and the acknowledgement and guarantee of differences: a long and civil process.

Dominion Day, July 1, 1867.

The Founding Fathers added "dominion" at the last moment to the country's title. Their first choice had been "kingdom", which they rejected because of its suggestion of an empire. Then they vetoed "republic" and "confederacy". Nevertheless, many representatives to the conferences said that "dominion" was obscure in its meaning, mostly ornamental, an extemporized name certain to be changed later. "It was rather absurd," sniffed the Earl of Derby, advisor to Benjamin Disraeli.

British politicians weren't much interested in Canada. The Prime Minister was preoccupied with domestic issues–particularly the Reform Bill that extended voting privileges to a larger British public–and distracted by Gladstone's ascension to the leadership of the Liberals. Political survival dominated Disraeli's mind.

And Queen Victoria's opinion of "dominion"? "Not a very happy addition," she said.

On the first Dominion Day, people spontaneously erected signs of celebration. Fireworks and outdoor concerts and welcoming orations and unfurled banners. Many of the signs conveyed a provocative, even a subversive, inconsistency in their messages. In Nova Scotia, people put back a word that had been vetoed by the Founding Fathers:

SUCCESS TO THE CONFEDERACY

And in Quebec:

BIENVENUE À LA NOUVELLE
PUISSANCE

The signs were loaded with meanings. There are overtones, layers. A confederacy means those who league together, join in a covenant; in short, a federation. It wouldn't have been lost on the international observers in 1867, a short time after the American Civil War and less than a hundred years after the War of Independence, that the word heralds rebels and rebellion, and not a revolution. "Puissance" links to the

English "puissant", meaning powerful; its etymology bridges, through the Italian "possente", to "potent". The word-echo for potent is indirect, significant: it is "possible".

Thursday, March 9, 1876.

The Exeter Place Laboratory, Boston, Massachusetts.

Alexander Graham Bell, resident of Brantford, Ontario, and Thomas Watson, Bell's assistant and a native of Salem, Mass., worked together to discover a method for transmitting the human voice through the air.

They studied sound waves, wires, membranes, tubing, the mysterious current. Bell and Watson dipped needles into water inside black boxes. They hoped that reed receivers would relay their voices.

Their experiments failed, but they persisted. "I could hear a confused muttering sound like speech," Bell wrote in his notebook, "but I could not make out the sense."

Bell's lifelong obsession was hearing. His wife, Mabel, was deaf; his father, Melville, pioneered a system for teaching the deaf. It was called Visible Speech (still in use today). Bell spent the principal part of his life in postures of listening. He paid close attention to what was said and left unsaid, to the rhythm of words, the arcane echoes of speech, and to silence. Thomas Watson claims in his memoir that he was a mystic, a medium who sought out occult meanings in seances and white magic rituals. It hadn't escaped him that he'd been raised in Salem, the site of the notorious witch trials. He felt the passion to listen, too.

Listening was an active and not a passive state for them. It was an act of acute, deep attentiveness. Listening meant picking up subtle vibrations and overtones. They made themselves receptive to voices issued from the other side of what they took to be reality. One scientist worked to restore a lost sense to the deaf; the other wanted to open channels to the netherworld. And to truly hear–to say, "I have heard"–means following your heart's beat.

Friday, March 10, 1876.

The two men tested a brass pipe, a platinum needle, and a box with a speaking-tube mouthpiece. Bell and Watson then went to separate rooms. They closed two doors between them. Their ensuing exchange is legendary.

The story says that these were the first words muttered over the line:

"Mr. Watson, come here. I want to see you."

Other accounts differ. Bell and Watson contradict one another in their notes and records, their retelling and reimaginings. After the moment of discovery, the first vocal communication through an electrical current, the two scientists couldn't agree on what they actually said.

Variations say:

"Come here, Watson, I need you."
"Mr. Watson, come here, I want you."

Watson returned, charged with excitement. Now it was his turn to speak. Legend has not chosen to preserve his utterance. But it is essential to recall it, too.

"Mr. Bell, do you understand what I say? Do-you-un-der-stand-what-I-say?"

Bell did hear, and he did understand.
The telephone was born.
Bell and Watson had indirectly discovered that no walls or closed doors, no barriers or barricades, can truly arrest the electric flux, the sometimes seismic circuits of energy, once we tap into them. These energy fields can tear down and build up rapidly. We may manage and influence, and try to canalize and even buffer, their urges and leaps, fluctuations and ripples, but we cannot stop the flow.

A cry for help, a call for connection and consultation. The calls that speak of a need for understanding. The crying out that hopes that comfort will come.

Bell supposedly spilled acid on himself, then squirming in pain and shock he called for his assistant to come to him. This story may be apocryphal, the result of Watson's imaginative retelling in his memoirs. It is the version that school children are taught, and it is the version that we hear through anecdote and see in movies and TV documentaries.

My point is this: the first words heard over the airwaves were a call for assistance. A Canadian inventor spoke to his American co-worker. Both then became confused about what was said.

"Do-you-un-der-stand-what-I-say?"

Help and comprehension, a voice asking for attention, a voice asking for confirmation that a communiqué has been received. People calling to each other; voices that make the attempt to bridge our solitudes, to bring solace.

Bell and Watson knew that the telephone would operate on the principle of sympathetic vibrations.

And in the reverberation of their breakthrough, the electric wires buzzed with a vulnerable message, urgent tones and ambiguous words, the pitch of vital minds and their insistent urge to discover meaning, the track of emotion, the search to find a sympathetic pulse and echo in other people and in the world.

Signal Hill, Newfoundland, December 12, 1901.

Guglielmo Marconi was flying a kite in a storm. After his receiving towers had been smashed down by the wind, he'd improvised by attaching an antenna to the kite and letting it soar. He was determined to prove that over-the-horizon reception was possible, that radio waves would follow the curvature of the earth and defy Euclidean law.

Marconi's kite endured the storm's blast. He'd arranged with associates in England to have a wireless message sent across the ocean. Shortly after 12:30 PM, his assistants in Cornwall telegraphed that message.

A single letter filtered through the squall.

"S . . ."

Three clicks, in Morse code.

Marconi listened on an earphone to the pulses that leapt from 3,300 km away. He'd become the first person to hear the other side of the world. His experiments proved that radio waves would travel long-distance without wires. Unseen power lines could crisscross the globe, the energies looking for receivers.

The intercontinental message was limited to a fragment: S. Out of fragments come implications. Symbolists would say that S stands for the snake of energy, the serpent of the cosmos, the power of life to recharge itself, and endure. In the mystic understanding of the world, the letter S is identified with lunar influence and tides, and the balancing of opposites. Turn the S on its side, complete the figure to make it resemble the figure eight, and you discover the symbol for infinity. S also symbolizes waves, their undulating form, their transient shape. It is, finally, the letter that evokes the constant hiss of electromagnetism, the sound of nature's energy, once again both waves and field.

Newfoundland did not join Confederation until 1949. Nevertheless, Signal Hill in St. John's has entered the mythology of a country obsessed with methods of communication linkage. On Signal Hill, an Italian inventor demonstrated that wireless messages would zigzag over the sea, thus extending ourselves into the atmosphere, allowing access to other languages, symbols, places, and sounds, filling the air with the human tone.

And air is the element of lightness.

Canadians quickly embraced radio technology. Across the country, teenagers built their own crystal sets, and discovered that the night was the best time for reception. They were probing the dark with their copper-wire feelers, hearing distant tinny voices. In 1920, the radio presence in Canada was confirmed by the first world broadcast of live music by CFCX in Montreal. Their programming only included music–and weather reports.

The pattern:

One communication story outlines the shape of civility, of tact and trust, of a recognition of the other (of difference, a necessary strangeness), and of an unusual partnership formed in a loose, mostly peaceable confederation. This is the story-line that emerges when we look at how the Fathers of Confederation gathered and welcomed debate on nation-building. That process stressed the lack of definition, the improvisational nature, of the agreement they called, with careful understatement, the BNA Act.

The other stories outline how we have tapped into energy sources and resources, spheres of influence, emanating powers that allowed and inspired the invention and proliferation of communication technologies. We see experimenters working to discover ways of reaching others, even of allowing the miraculous cosmos to speak through us, pulling from the air live traditions. Through the confusions and often mixed motives of the experimenters, came higher ways of communicating, of enlarging how much we can actually say or deliver to one another.

Encounters and valedictions, summons and replies: the communication of meaning implies an act of the heart, an openness that may lead to embarrassment and pain, muddle and contention; but that communication also trusts that something will come, something essential will be passed on between people, between the cosmos and ourselves.

Discovery, experimentation, confusion, error, the tensions of wildness and order–these factors are part of what evolves here. The communications stories show developing technologies and memoranda, and their gradual convergence into the data-rush we have come to witness and admit. And they show the longing for connection, to be participants in a creation.

Sir Wilfrid Laurier said, in a well-known statement, "The twentieth century belongs to Canada." Again these words are layered with ambiguities, meanings Laurier himself no doubt didn't intend. The word "belong" links to the Medieval English *langian,* meaning to crave for, to long after. Of course, Laurier's statement suggests a golden future awaits the Canadian experiment. But it does not necessarily suggest the expansions of empire. The statement hints that Canada will provide a civilized foundation on which modernity can work out a destiny that differs from other fresh-born societies.

I've juxtaposed the Fathers of Confederation and Wilfrid Laurier with Alexander Graham Bell, Thomas Watson and Guglielmo Marconi to show how Canada is an experiment in an alternative current. I call it a communication state: this is the condition of receptivity, the pattern of listening and dialogue and misunderstanding, of broken messages and missed connections, of perpetual mediation and trial through technology, of reading the signs and scanning for signals.

The only way we can live in this country is through advanced technologies of communication. We need the telephone, the telegraph, the radio, the satellite dish, TV, and the computer, air travel and trains. The paradox is that these technologies do not solidify individual identity; they do not focus a singular identity for any one person. Electricity scatters individual memory, conjuring ghostly simulations. It transmits static, shards of disconnected data, pieces of a riddle that may be in itself part of a greater enigma. Tribes, clubs, corporations, and cults can arise from the power-flow from TV sets, radios, telephones, computer networks: the isolated individual's need for meaning can sometimes translate into an insidious handing of power over to a larger group. Yet electronic technologies spur and excite questions, allow for multiple points of view, add to the strange feeling of fusion with world events and confusion about significance and intent. Communication technologies threaten us, summon us, immerse us: they appear to be capable of dehumanizing our lives and of enhancing our awareness, sending out images and reflections of ourselves everywhere.

In electric city, we are haunted by a sense of presence, the trace of something close, almost there. Is that presence supernatural, otherworldly, or is it our human world amplified, echoing, calling, yearning, crying out? Could it be both? The electroscape is a realm of emanations and radiance, music and mystery.

Debate and energy, a country established over a bargaining table, a myth made out of vibrations in the air.

I believe that Canada has a hermetic past: its meanings are concealed in private whisperings and interrupted signals, in insoluble arguments about unity and misread messages, and in quiet resistance to the pressure to join into one supreme, monolithic political system. I suggest that Canada has a discontinuous, contradictory character. I mean that without a single purpose or predetermined historic goal–no violent creation and imposition of a homogenous political myth or ideology–Canadians have lived with, invited, and responded to paradox, to many stories, moods and visions, and to many different kinds of people and voices.

Patterns only become clear in an overview, in that instant when levels of reality stand revealed. The Canadian patterns often look obscure to visitors, so we stoop to define ourselves through what we are not (neither American nor British). The communications stories hint that the Canadian space has always been a through-zone, adaptable and reflective, a medium through which questions, calls, pulses, and ideas pass.

The historian Arthur Lower is said to have commented that Canada's strength is its anonymity. An often-quoted and reworked remark. Like so many Canadian figures, A.R.M. Lower led a double life: he wrote humorous squibs under the pseudonym, L.E.G. Upper. The comment attributed to the almost forgotten Lower has endured. People often say that we are faceless, we blend in easily, disappearing into unfamiliar environments. When people stereotype others into distinct national personae–the gregarious American, the aloof French, the contemptuous British–they speak of the quiet Canadian, the unassuming voyager in the world-body politic.

I'll adapt Lower's remark and call the anonymity part of our invisibility, our chameleon nature. Quietness outside, dynamism within. We have in Canada unofficially acknowledged three founding peoples–British, French, and Aboriginal; we admit to multicultural influences. Yet writers and media commentators cannot say what a Canadian is. Our identities are kept hidden, like diary entries that no one is meant to read but whose meaning is clear to their author.

We recognize secret sides to ourselves. Our most mythologized political leaders–say Wilfrid Laurier, Mackenzie King, John Diefenbaker, Pierre Trudeau–exude fascination because their characters, motives, and actions remain complex, unfathomable. When literary critics referred to the one true Canadian theme of the bush, or survival–an outgrowth of the ideology of cultural nationalism in the 1960s–we were apt to nod our heads and say, "Well, maybe…" The sixties' nationalists concerned themselves with questions of identity, definition. But we continue to glimpse through guesses, hunches, rumours, and intimations, that our deepest resource is in flux and inner lives, something which is quixotic, tentative, sometimes withdrawn, exploratory, in a process that refuses finished explanation and a fixed content.

It may be that we know how the anonymous Canadian, who lives in a place where communication links are a matter of air and vibrations and hints and crossed wires, has no need for a static identity. It may be that this anti-nation, our eclectic mosaic culture, this condition of being seemingly disparate and separate (distinct society provisions within the whole society; regional tensions; the virtual city-state that is now Toronto; aboriginal landclaims), all our obsessions with who we are, may be our strength, our promising path, our myth, an original form of harmony.

A multiple and mobile perspective is vital for perceiving the effects of electric city. In the electronic culture of speeding and disruptive bits of information, ideological rigidity, and schematic theories, dialectical imperatives and dogma may help us to make reality temporarily clear, but the truth of our lives is variety, paradox, concealed destinies, interconnection, latent forms. Lewis Thomas writes about the data deluge in *The Lives of a Cell* evoking the rush of images and bytes:

> Somewhere, obscured by the snatches of conversation, pages of old letters, bits of books and magazines, memories of old movies, and the disorder of radio and television, there ought to be more intelligible signals. Or perhaps we are only at the beginning of learning to use the system, with almost

all of our evolution... still ahead
of us...

Canadians, I've said, appear to be capable of
wearing masks, capable of flexible positions and
improvised responses. Some say this is bland;
others call it tact and civility, a high order of
polite civilization. I say that it's a realistic understanding of what it means to exist in the global
society, the planetary culture, where private
identity must be cloaked if it's to maintain solitude, measures of integrity and mystery.

Esoteric writings speak of veiled destiny,
cryptic codes, and the spiritual transmutation of
the self. Who are we? the alchemists asked: an
amorphous, mystifying harmony of divisions, of
contradictions and qualities, each person a
microcosm of heaven and hell, of angelic and
demonic conflict. So the mystic philosophers
wanted us to find the still-point of meaning
inside ourselves, the stillness within, the point of
self-transcendence, the centre of our true being
from where we always depart, to which we can
return. Esoteric language is richly imaginative
and metaphoric: it expresses the essential desire
for personal transformation. Elusive intent, the

mining for gold, spirit, introspection: we search to know what is the best and worst in us, what can be transmuted into truths that yield patterns of possibility.

The communication philosophies that developed in Canada, the thinking of Harold Innis, George Grant, and Marshall McLuhan, pointed to the unfixed quality in the Canadian soul. Innis and Grant, drenched in tragic readings of history, reacted with foreboding and sorrow in their books. A state so vulnerable and anonymous could lose its bearings, become prey to the monopolies of the American empire. Grant said, "No small country can depend for its existence on the loyalty of its capitalists." McLuhan responded with his customary ambivalence, and with a hint of a future responsibility: he said that our unformed condition could be an informed one, a thoughtful position that could become both dangerous and infused with potential.

Questions linger: what will be the patterns that allow Canadians to go on into the future? We missed the vicious civil wars and liberating revolutions of nineteenth and early twentieth century nationalism. Is our loose federation a paradigm for the electric city of the teleworld? What could be the result of our bizarre symbiosis of technology and raw human need? Somewhere in the information boom, we've lost a wisdom that could be reclaimed. Canada may be fast-forwarding into a new pattern, a model of communication linkages, a civilization that is more than a grab for power and dominance, a place that can channel the fire of the global wiring, where political alliances are subject to electrical ebb and flow and the alchemical transformation of self may prevail over the ideology of capital.

I'll close this first meditation with thoughts on noise and data.

There are several possible etymologies for the word, "noise". One stresses the old French, the Provençal origins, "nauza", "noisa", "neuiza". Nausea and nauseous stem from these roots; noisome comes from them, too. The latter is an archaic word, which means troubling, irritating. Obviously, noise is something that can make you sick. I've found another echo, another reading. Noise may come from "nous", the Greek word for mind. From the same Greek root we get mood, mode, atmosphere, ambience, the tone of a time and place. Noise may be the roar of the age, voices on the verge of being heard, rhythms not yet fully registered, the shape of things to come. News always follows in the din. But the new is slightly out of the reach of our immediate grasp and responses.

Different kinds of noise sound in the air. One I call media junk, the strain of data, the clamour and hum of too many reports, communiqués, slogans, bulletins, opinions, experts' advice, consultants' templates, diagnoses, prognoses, accounts. Mystics speak of this tumult when they describe the soul's chatter that blocks out the patterns of spiritual practice and learning, which lead to concentration, and the hope of transcendence. Noise can also become a siren's call, a warning, a cry for help, the junk suddenly transforming into an expression of people's suffering and need. I call this news, the data of new voices stirring. These are the mutterings and low-frequency pulses of the language we don't know, the evolving articulation of facts, materials, myths, and symbols. When world models collide, stories of reality overlap.

Media noise is the result of an excess of TV, radio broadcasts, computer printouts, polls, muzak, headlines, statistics, and graphs. The mania of too much information, the mercilessness of disjointed input. A diffusion and oppression of your senses and ideas occurs when the images and bytes don't connect or cohere for you. People experience amnesia at that moment. Communication then becomes difficult, and authentic voices may vanish, be overwhelmed. Historical perspective vanishes into the spill of commercials, TV reruns, and ephemeral head-lines.

Inside the same dataflow, there may appear another set of messages. This is polyphony, the genuine plurality of different approaches and interpretations. Pluralism is not relativity. In the polyphony, every individual has one voice with which to speak, two ears with which to listen. Each voice carries a portion of the truth. No one person, government, ideology, or transnational can own and dominate the whole.

In our global culture, the chatter and input can tranquilize us, numb us, shear or warp our perceptions. Simultaneously, the blare and pressure may be the chaos out of which other structures of consciousness develop.

We live in a time of noisy nights and days. Like the nation-builders who sat down to talk, we have the opportunity to continue peacefully debating and arguing. Like Bell listening for his colleague, and like Watson listening for Bell, each of them doing so through closed doors and over makeshift wiring, we search for sympathetic vibrations, and what it means to listen to one another. Like Marconi with his improvised antenna, we work to receive the messages, to recognize the codes and patterns, and to supply and affirm the human tone.

I've said that I perceive communication to be the value of Canada. I believe this myth could move us in a multitude of directions. One story accelerates towards an economic-political crash, bafflement and frustration, disappointment in political leaders of whatever affiliation, a shut down of faith in the future, and people retreating behind the walls of ethnic and racial rivalries. Another story reveals the need for understanding, for people to find some way of bridging gaps and solipsisms. We share in the memory of the call for help over the airwaves: the vulnerability of the admission, that confession. And we've forgotten the story of the nation-builders who went on talking, despite their fears and scepticism, resentments and disagreements, and who knew that Canada's spirit was an improvisational, accommodating one.

Electronic technologies will sweep us into shocking patterns and unexpected relations. Every element in all the communications stories suggests that in this process of crack-up and discovery, the electric initiation, our country's lack of definition and codification—its lightness—could be its strength.

In the roar of their media-saturated environments, our politicians and leaders become deaf to the noise of the people they represent. These are the voices carrying the clues and indications that say:

Do—not—let—
our—experiment—
slip—
from—us—

INTERLUDE
On Justice

Questions. They keep coming and coming, over the air, onto our screens, through to us, into our minds and our daily concerns, more all the time. We sense how the wiring of the teleworld ignites and hums with crackling intensities and outcries, in some endless recharging of itself. Electrodynamism is not a thing, an object, but an enlarging pattern of actions and reactions. Thus we are being filled with errant vibrations, feeling the effects of energies passing over into us, and from us, receiving the almost preternatural sensation that unlimited communication now takes place.

*

Many forces drive the technologized borderless order. But the primary force, in these seedling moments where so much grows and spreads, appears to be the market, fuelled by fierce desire. Electrical fire and the fire of greed kindle economics. In that flux, capital runs amok, while nations become digitized commodities on stock-exchange floors–products to be rated for their obedience to paying off deficits and debts.

*

What is justice in this race? How do we pose ethical, spiritual considerations in the revved flow of jolted, nomadic economies?

*

Justice is living harmony–the marriage of opposites that creates the only balance we can know. But we engage and are engulfed by organizations that put economics first, displacing issues of the common good, of justice itself.

These are what I take to be the four keys to civilized life, humane existence: liberty; recognition of self-worth (which can be translated to mean service, or employment); universal health care; equality of opportunity. Those four keys honour the person. Any political-economic system, whether governed by parties of the right or of the left, which seeks to degrade or diminish the worth of a person, cannot be a spirit moving toward the fulfilment of the good.

*

But when technology finally penetrates or permeates all spheres of life, we have reason to fear that uniformity will be the result, and not wholeness. If the telephone was invented and constructed on the principle of sympathetic vibrations, then the dance of electricity guarantees that there will be a shadow effect that will accompany the invention–an effect which will show itself in an unsympathetic repercussion, a restriction on empathy and conscience, a narrowing down of perspective, a slamming shut of the doors of perception.

*

We can know more, feel more, in the electrodynamism of the planetary city, sometimes whether we wish to or not. To protect what may be the deep rule of things–the harmony of conflicts–we must pose probing and receptivity against numbness, a courageous gentleness against ferocity and cruelty, sweetness and strength against skinless intolerance, justice against growing inequities.

There must still be engagement; there must still be protest.

LETTER TO THOSE
IN POWER

If the leaders of mankind were more aware, when by chance they come into minor powers they might exploit others less.

From *The Gateless Gate*,
a collection of koans first recorded
by a Chinese master in AD 1228

To those in power,

How do I address a mindset? How do I challenge and criticize what is in fact becoming the global paradigm, a dogmatic line that slashes across ideological alliances, a model so pervasive few genuinely oppose it? Who is there to answer for the desensitizing, the "adapt or perish" economic survivalism, the abstractions that drug and dull the language of trade, the apotheosis of technology so that it becomes the answer rather than a part of the human question and quest, the equation of free markets with democracy and true liberty, that we encounter in almost every system? If the transnational corporations are the decisive players of the global society, are there even individuals left to address? Again, how do I talk to a collective, a state of mind?

The corporate-economic model of our lives, our society, governs us. Economists, mostly in the pay of the transnationals, appear to be deciding what democracy is, and will be. There are, and have been, political advocates of the economy-first mindset–Brian Mulroney and Preston Manning in Canada, Newt Gingrich in the United States, Margaret Thatcher in England–but these speakers on behalf of the politics of the bottomline do not always appear to directly represent or embody the forces shaping, rearranging our choices, our values. To be incorporated means to belong to one body—to be absorbed, or swallowed. Commentators and analysts say we are experiencing today a crisis in government and leadership, in how we can govern and lead. I believe our crisis is a spiritual one. How do we find light; how will we see; what are we listening to; what do our hearts say; who is speaking to us. We have handed management and influence over to market strategists and the transnationals who can afford the new technologies. But their value is not human beings, or the struggle of the soul to balance or transcend its shadow; their value is only the course of profit. The market always sparks invention, of course. What differs now is the ascendancy of the market without a counterbalancing critique or philosophical option. The system, the mindset, in short, is out of whack. And a tyranny occurs when we can find no way out.

How can anyone, how can we, shift our view of reality away from the consensual hallucination called deficit and debt reduction?

Those in power have given authority to the corporatist-collective mind, which is supported by the inflamed organisms of electronic technology.

Here, then, is the flipside, the reverse angle, of the Canada of light: the flexible confederation, with its communications story, becomes vulnerable to a transnational despotism. We stand at the beginning of what could be the most human century, a renaissance of wonders–culture, science, commerce, politics, and communication joining together–and we feel and experience the terror and ecstasy, the trauma and learning, that erupt in the confusion. But what we call "nationhood", or "sovereignty", no longer appears to describe, or evoke, our rattled and fluid state.

And for us, one question must rise above the others: what will it cost us to remain Canadian in the global marketplace?

The economic survivalism that possesses us elevates the market to a first principle. But surely we must ask, what is the supposed freeflow of wealth for? who profits? is there a direction in the borderless economy, where everything runs everywhere? If massive trading systems are a necessity—which they no doubt are—then what will happen to the experiment called Canada, the alternative current, when it is melded, or diffused?

Economics are about states of mind, about moods. Always I try to translate these abstract, often baffling processes back into humane terms, into a language I can myself comprehend. And I see this: with the market raised to a first principle, we guarantee the mindlessness of the financial enterprise; we guarantee its complete lack of civil guidance, of kindness. "Kind": meaning character, and sympathy, generosity and benevolence; from the source word "kin", or "kindred", meaning affinity and relationship. "Kind" suggests the knowledge that what we do must affect and move the soul. Thus the crisis of government of which we hear so much must be a crisis of deep connection and imagination.

In Canada, we have watched our governments, provincial and federal, participate in the merging of the market with ruling. And in this merger we have observed these mostly unquestioned assumptions surface and dominate:

Drop the walls of government regulation, dismantle what are perceived to be unprofitable Crown corporations, drive issues of governing and political responsibility away from questions of injustice, inequality, ethics, dehumanization and oppression, exalt consumption, push questions of citizenship away from the broad public sphere into the narrowed zones of homes and neighbourhoods and therefore limit the individual's influence on the overall system (make individuals in fact feel that they can't have much of an influence at all), promote the language of trade and markets over the language of inspiration (of compassion and comprehension, of spirit and common humanity) so that people feel embarrassed and uncomfortable when they hear any argument that is not considered realistic, enhance the mobility of capital through improved global communications, hand more power over to unelected officials in institutions like the IMF and the World Bank, provoke and maintain the fear that we will somehow lose "most favoured nation status" with money lenders and currency speculators, make power the ultimate act of consumption, make massive cutbacks in the areas where people need more development (in the organization of services, in education and health, in the arts and scientific research, in the infrastructure of society), change the symbolism of Canada from a place with a distinctive though enigmatic and perhaps shrouded evolutionary spirit and character to an investment property for fast sale.

Every movement must have its manifesto. I found one in *A New Direction for Canada: An Agenda for Economic Renewal*, which was presented to the House of Commons by the Honourable Michael H. Wilson, Finance Minister, on November 8, 1984. Colour this paper blue. And blue, the symbolists say, is darkness made visible.

We find the corporatist *perestroika* in Wilson's paper, the outline for the future. In Wilson's introduction, we discover projections, plans, hypotheses, and deductions, the call for review. Here the machine–mind exposes itself; here begins the rule of international bureaucrats in Canada.

I quote randomly from the text:

"… expansive, intrusive government…"

"… an economic world that had changed and a country that had not kept pace with that change…"

"... the inherent dynamism of Canadians and Canadian business has been eroded by economic policies which, though often well-intentioned, have been erratic, have discouraged productivity..."

The first pages signal that the target of the government attack will be the debt. Wilson lambastes

"... regulation and intervention..."

He raises "the judgement of those in the marketplace" to the highest order. He claims that nothing less than a complete "economic reconstruction" will suffice to pull Canada back from the abyss of bankruptcy. To whom does Wilson answer? He speaks of foreign investors, unnamed speculators who will not pronounce Canada to be a sound commodity until the government follows the policies of deregulation and undertakes drastic measures.

I quote again from his declaration:

"... Failure to control our deficit when others are controlling theirs would undermine confidence..."

"... a revitalization of the private sector as the driving force behind growth and job creations..."

"... new competitive realities in the world marketplace..."

"... government subsidies have distorted market signals..."

"... government services and activities, either directly or through crown corporations, are needlessly supplanting private entrepreneurship...

"... government has become too big..."

Then I discovered a passage written four years before the Free Trade debate erupted and threatened to snap the country in two, long before Prime Minister Mulroney said anything in public about dropping trade barriers, and before he made promises about "sacred trusts". Wilson plants his land-mine:

"... if we are to foster growth through trade, we must obtain more secure and improved access to foreign markets on the broadest possible basis. This would require, of course, that Canada would also have to move to increase access to its domestic market..."

Wilson mildly describes "the adjustment that freer trade would entail…" There will be a lot of talk about this "adjustment".

Wilson's demand for the government to review every role it plays in the economy ricochets from these pages. Via Rail, The National Energy Program, Petro-Canada, the Foreign Investment Review Agency, Child Benefits, Unemployment Insurance, benefits to the elderly… all that we have called our infrastructure. Despite the assurances of the Mulroney-Wilson government that social policies were never on the negotiating table, these pages explosively prove that they were from the start.

I'll give Wilson his due. He asks hard questions, phrases problems realistically. He thinks like a tough-minded banker, or an overly ambitious accountant. There are, he insists, "the limits of budgetary realities…" He informs us that "some of the changes necessary for an economic turnaround are strong medicine…" If Wilson hints at the levying of a new sales tax, he says so in bland terms, telling us the raising revenues "by other means" may be necessary. He may have been a prophetic figure: the first of what has since become a succession of accountants and auditors turned politicians.

In "Goals", Wilson explicitly states how the Progressive Conservative government under Mulroney must limit government, transfer the cost of social programs to the provinces, reduce interference in the actions of transnationals, increase the self-reliance of individuals, establish the free-enterprising policies which will attract foreign investors.

The blueprint couldn't have been clearer. Why were we never told? Yes, Wilson read his manifesto in the House of Commons: he undoubtedly delivered it in his monotonous boardroom style, a manner so detached and dispassionate that only the most obsessive critic would stay awake to pay attention. Boredom can be a strategy for politicians. Make things sound inoffensive and dull, and no one will listen.

I recall that Mulroney distanced himself from the clarion call of the corporate people. He said this bluepaper merely contained suggestions, recommendations. He would never undermine the achievements of Canadian society, wouldn't alter the structure of the social security net. I don't recall that we had an election on all the proposals and precepts of the Wilson formula. Yet these

words–for all their mandarin tone and bureaucratic gentility–shout out.

I'll quickly review the corporatist tenets:

the free market is absolutely good;
government interference is bad, always inept;
the deficit is always the problem;
we are entirely answerable to international currency speculators and market analysts;
we must compete in the global marketplace by immediately merging into a North American trade block.

Wilson implies the question: can we afford Canada? If you agree with the logic of his bluepaper, then your answer would have to be no: Canada makes no economic sense whatsoever. If you make linear economics the single basis of your thinking, then there is no good reason to pursue an individualized experiment north of the 49th parallel. We simply cannot afford it.

But reality becomes murky in the Wilson blueprint. His advisors provide him with statistics, forecasts, percentages. Numbers push and crowd. Graphs chart dips and swells of financial speculation. Long lists mix with mathematical figures. Prophecies predict narratives of boom and bust. I was barraged by arcane diagrams—analyses of the future.

This is a report based on economists' virtual models. It is the result of minds mesmerized by screens and numbers, by reams of statistics and the flash of computer speed, the electrons and digits of the pulsing 1s and 0s. Anyone who thinks outside the specialized realm of economists will be baffled.

The Wilson blueprint conjures a graph projection out of facts, figures, and guesswork. Experts and their on-screen flowcharts can easily hypnotize those who are eager for an absolute answer to their problems or questions. *A New Direction for Canada* is a kind of science fiction: it is what the economists think will happen.

I read the Wilson manifesto with a growing sense of recognition. This mindset dominates us through most of our politicians, regardless of party. Over the past decade, we have witnessed the signing of the Free Trade Agreement with the United States, the de-indexing of old-age pensions, the elimination of the possibility of government-funded childcare, cutbacks in

Canada Assistance Plan funding, the GST controversy, the passing of NAFTA in the House of Commons; we have experienced the effects of record high unemployment across the country, a burgeoning national debt, the emergence of an enraged workforce.

What looked like the removal of domineering government forces became the abdication of government responsibility. What was supposed to be an agenda of renewal became the politics of deal-making and retrenchment, of slash and burn.

This manifesto must be the first political polemic ever written in the passive voice. I'm speaking of bureaucratic prose, the use of the linking verb and the absence of an I or a we, the avoidance of an authentic personal presence.

Depersonalized language hints that no one can be held responsible for what's said and done. "Employment will do this...", Wilson's bluepaper announces. "Expenditures reductions will be difficult..." "The government attaches top priority..." "Concern has been expressed..." The document's pages ooze with departmental grease. Make it smooth, easy. Blend anything personal into the apparent omniscient force of mass technology.

I see the emotional severing in the blueprint. The cold prose obscures the harsh rearrangements. The corporatist gospel does not reveal how there must be loss, hurt, disarray, perplexity. They do not say that their proposals are a pseudo-scientific projection from computer-generated models. The objective tone masks how this is only one group of people talking, offering its opinion.

With the use of the passive voice in the government blueprint, we see a triumph of the corporate mind and virtual models over the individual's tone and imagination—over responsiveness, intuition, attentiveness, and flexibility. With the mathematical abstractions of deficits and GNPs, we see a triumph of structure over personality, of the economic mindset over the quality of life. During a time of shifting world paradigms—the move from industrial mechanism to electric sensation and digital simulation—we must ask for a visionary pragmatism from our politicians and leaders, an engagement that emerges from the debate about values, the principles of power, the complexities of influence, the spending of our wealth.

But the Wilson blueprint declared that the enemy of the people is the government. And this was a representative of the government speaking. How ironic, and how suicidal. How contrary to the history of Canada, with its tradition of a balance between public and private roles. I challenge the corporatist assumption. In a planetary culture of entwined economies, of people communicating across borderlines through the electronic media, where data hurtles and jams at the speed of light, where we live bathed in TV emanations and radio waves, how can we say that government will always be the enemy of the people? Government can be authoritarian, brutal; it can be monolithic, static, and stupid, of course. But obedience to the corporatist call has led us to this point: a breakdown of trust in what people in government can do.

Leaders often speak of the cynicism and sourness of Canadians. I hear people speak about the disconnection from human affairs in those who govern. It may be that the people feel this way because Canada had once been an example of a state where government was necessary for the survival of the country's social structure.

I read through the numbers and platitudes of the Wilson manifesto, and I recalled how the Mulroney government, and all subsequent governments, have shielded themselves in statistics, polls, graphs, percentages, censes, the seemingly innocuous terminology of "adjustment". When I looked closely at the characterless style of the bluepaper, I kept asking: who runs the state? and who is the state for?

We appear to have yielded our cultural-political destiny, our unfolding story, to the codes of the anonymous mass organizations who go under the names of GATT and NAFTA. We are governed for "the benefit of foreign interests." Our own leaders have helped to unravel the careful arrangement of checks, the balance, established between previous regimes, between government and transnationals and unions, between small businesses and academies and the mass media. Government has retreated from its mediation role in our society.

(When Canada joined NAFTA, a small economy melded into the most powerful one in the world. There are few similarities between our situation and that of the European Common Market, where old cultures, tested and defined over aeons, exist in strong, although uneasy, partnerships.)

Political and business leaders are responsible for policy and indirectly responsible for the moods and emotions of a place and time.

Through legislation, public acts, speeches and gestures, a political leader can affect both the economy and the cultural and moral life of a country.

What is the perception that many people have of those in power, and of the effects of business and political leadership on our moods?

It is one of absence, of automatic actions, of compulsion, and the uttering of clichés. It is of directions that were not vividly imagined, honestly debated, prepared for, and constantly reevaluated. We find ourselves asking questions about authenticity in cyber-economics because the issues of justice appear to have been shoved aside. We see the inability of governments to respond to rapid metamorphosis, and thus we see rulers who cannot listen to the scramble and desperation of those who have been discarded by the fissions and transfers of the borderless order. Prolonged recession has become a euphemism for depression. We see governments setting deficit control and lean fiscal operations over fairness, equity–creation of conditions where support can be scaled back without loss of opportunity or dignity. The main streets of the planetary city veer everyday into mean streets. Free Trade appears to push down wages, push up profits; the few benefit, many do not. (One political observer recently called NAFTA "a race to the bottom.") When governments slash into programs in the name of financial reform and tax cuts, they invariably tear into the funding that maintains roads, trains, schools, Medicare, welfare, airports, the post office, public buildings, museums, art galleries, publishing houses, symphonies, theatres. When we chronicle those in power, we see many politicians succumbing to the corporatist mindset, sometimes finding themselves using the machine-speak of desensitized language. We have witnessed in Canada several Prime Ministers who said they would strengthen the Canadian federal experiment, and then allowed what has always been a dark prospect to come out of the murky atmosphere: complete economic assimilation into the United States.

We have released ourselves to wander the world through electrical connection–lightflyers, lightgliders, who know the cool air and white wonder of the north. If this is so, then surely a new deal should accompany our evolution. With expanded consciousness must come acute responsiveness.

When I find myself observing those who lead us, I struggle to put a face to the global mindset.

What sort of people are they? Who are they? The market is wasteful of individuals; it certainly knows little of kindness, or compassion. What it demonstrates is vital hunger and need, certainly a remarkable ingenuity. But when I observe and examine our leaders in most political parties, I sense something missing in them. Something empty in them. Many elected officials and business leaders show admirable traits of toughness; they can bob and weave, and they can take a punch—though punch-drunk boxers eventually lose their timing and misread their circumstances. Some are dogged campaigners, canny tacticians. They may even be sincere.

Our politicians and business leaders are not evil people, nor even especially venal. But their goodness has little will, or spirit; it does not seem to enlarge them. And without a grasp of human suffering, the moral realities, the dilemmas and riddles of everyday existence, they become denatured–the word Edmund Burke once used to describe politicians who have no awareness of what effect their actions have on others. The global mindset, conditioned by financial logic, has lost its imagination.

What I mean by this is the loss of the ability to perceive difference, to sympathize with suffering and muddle, weakness and fear, to feel for people and what they do and can't do. The economic mindset seems incapable of transcending the hypnotism of geometry and categorical solution, "Single vision and Newton's sleep," in Blake's words. The imagination is the key to the spirit, to empathy, to seeing pattern in incongruity, to reclaiming cohesiveness, to augury and omen, to the realm of soulful questioning and contemplation of our mystery, to recognizing that there is always a person behind every word, in every place, on every street, in every situation. The imagination seals us in a covenant with the world; it takes the world back into ourselves, inspiring us to know more—to find more rhymes, synchronicities, those endless connections that ring us. Without that visionary inkling, which is the mind's openness to alternatives, we will be in Canada a country without strangeness, little more than another greedy place, a seething and frustrating and perhaps eventually vicious society, another spot on the map torn apart by insidious ignorance and myopia, another footnote to the saga of the United States, some minor addendum to other histories and destinies.

What makes the leadership of many so discomfiting to the people is their rule by will and necessity alone. Their actions and speeches indicate a failure to imagine what the effects of their words, gestures, promises, and policies will be.

Those in power seem to relish circulating in the insular scenes of political-economic abstractions. Clearly, it's been important for our leaders to side with the powerful, the international money interests, the corporate alliances and lobbyists, the in-club managers of world-wide organizations. We receive impressions of rulers set only in the mould of ambition, incapable of emotional or spiritual growth. And when we observe the figures who appear on the global stage, scanning them through TV irradiations, we sometimes seem to be seeing data, structures that have somehow become virtually independent of lives, of raw living—the corporation itself becoming a life form.

TV can mercilessly, sometimes ecstatically, expose us. Its rays will disclose and exalt the lines, marks, shapes, and shadows in a face. The cathode gun behind the screen can brighten and inform the human appearance, probing and recasting our features and expressions, as if this instrument were at times beginning to uncannily offer something greater than spectacle and diversion. TV seems, in occasional brilliant spots, to transmit glimpses of our souls—in a blinding metaphysical instant. What TV may have divulged about those in power is the divorce between thoughts and feelings. TV has X-rayed the rule by will and necessity alone.

But the images and sound bites also record and replay, imprint, and display, the faces and voices of people who have been hurt, frightened, lost, left distraught and unprotected. The electronic media can broaden and deepen feelings of dislocation, sensations of alarm. Electricity makes many angles intimate to us, opening up homes to multichannel communiqués and subliminal noise, transfiguring cathode light. All life breathes inside our living rooms. Scenes spin by, with music and rumours and talk and slow-motion highlights, paradigms of chaos and ancient myths fusing, becoming familiar and revelatory, beautiful and terrifying.

While those in government and in the transnationals try to confirm renewal, the end of the recession, what people feel and identify in others is psychic depression. The media has quickly illuminated, in intensive beams and high frequencies, the crucial story of worry and fatigue.

What is the cost of being Canadian? The Wilson manifesto answers with the phrases "sound economy", "fiscal responsibility". This answer has become one obsessed with interest rates, market competitiveness and consumption. I don't doubt the importance of these issues. But no individual, no people, no society or country, will find meaning and transcendence, an imaginative reason for being, if the answer is only economic. The corporatist answer disregards any recognition of how Canada differs from other states, and all questions of the good, that deeper responsiveness to our emotions and needs, experiences and values.

The transnationalist legacy imposes this message on us:

Everything is for sale, strip down, travel fast, enshrine the marketplace, be hard, give up your time, join the club, serve anyone who will give you the best deal, rush into signing those deals, travel faster, treat all institutions—from universities to hospitals—as if they were the same corporation, make sure that all politicians become ruthless about deficit cutting, face that life is about how much you make and how much you spend but in the end find yourself dependent on the fortunes and failures of the transnationals themselves and not the self-reliant individual that economic manifestos and blueprints encourage.

Without imagination, without inspiration, those in power have often been mesmerized by the transnational elites of privilege and influence. And so they have lost the chance to command our cultural stories and legacies, the spirits and concealed currents of our society. They have lost the chance to govern bonded with the individual citizen who must persevere, make sacrifices, pay the bills, dream of a better future, of a life that carries the possibility of vitality and enlightenment.

I set out to write this in the form of a letter. It was meant to be addressed to our politicians and business leaders. I had thought about singling out an individual–some specific politician, perhaps a Minister of Finance, or an IMF repre-sentative. Now I'm not sure where I would send it, and to whom. Such is the effect of the corpo-ratist model. Eventually, you begin to think in mass terms.

I'm also arrested by the notion that left-wing and right-wing economists share this concept: all culture is superstructure–peripheral; that which you can afford only when you have the money. I take the imagination, that mix of vision and reality, to be the starting point of all human endeavour. Culture must enfold eco-nomics, or there will be little purpose or direc-tion to the amassing of wealth, and to how that wealth is distributed. Economic survivalism rapes dignity. But the answer is not more or less government, or even better government. The answer comes in the reversal, the change of a state of mind–transforming the course of the money mind to that of humane perception, the prizing of the person, of the soul. If this view became our reality, then the imagination of those who rule and shape the channels of wealth would be released from slavery, servitude to mechanism, the logic of the machine, the mesmerism of the screen. Culture preserves civilization society. If there is no inspiration, then the political economy becomes nothing more than a heedless, insensate reflection of all the potencies in electrodynamism.

To the corporate mindset,

You have misunderstood how politics and governing are also about the spark of the spirit and transcendent insight, the way we envision and remould reality. You misread the complex moods of people, their strivings and anxieties. Politics is not only about policy and fiscal restraint, it involves myth and magic; it concerns emotion and perception, ideas and aspirations, how we respond to the dreams of people, what we each love, ponder, yearn for, fear, and desire, the best that is in us. Again, I say that you have cut yourselves off from the roots of the imagination. And like someone incubated in a laboratory cell, your temperature regulated by the purposes of the transnationals, for whom all light must mean the glare of publicity, you have lived unconsciously, disconnected from the feelings and hopes of others, lacking in sharp-edged growth, the stirring and unfolding of the soul, thus leaving few traces behind you of your heart.

Now we find we must begin again to listen to stories of the other new land, the indefinable place, whose elusive spirit is still forming. Canada may be the *via media,* the middle way, between the United States and Europe. We must find that route again, and follow it, to see where the whispering path may lead.

INTERLUDE
On the Secret Country

"We can't live on poetry alone," the currency speculators say.

I answer: "No, but nor can we live without it."

The Trojan Wars without Homer, it has been said, were nothing more than a battle over trade routes. We need the wind and air of metaphor, myth, lyrical language, verbal music, to help shift our mood, to tip the balance back, away from the primary focus on economic heat, toward just relations.

Sometimes it seems we have lost the ability to sing.

And there are fires other than those which can consume us.

*

Here is where I find myself: I have to explore what can be heard and viewed again in the auroras of our hidden-away Canada, the secret country where solitude and peace still largely exist, where we can ask questions about injustices and imbalances, about whether there is a vocation in being Canadian, hoping against hope, expecting the impossible. Yet there is no map for this secret country because–to echo a line of Thomas Merton's–it is within ourselves.

When we try to address reality, life, it is like pointing our fingers at the lights of the aurora borealis. The hand making the gesture is not truly important: it is the phenomenon we need to see, to comprehend. But the aurora borealis remains mysterious, always beyond our grasp. The essential thing is to point to that something beyond us.

*

Above the din, we listen for other music. Beyond the dimming, we strive for light. This is what we must continue to do when the Arctic lights sometimes seem curtained off, and when the voices of the other new land are quiet.

SECOND MEDITATION
The Alternative Current

I was now working with that occult force, electricity, and here was a possible chance to make some discoveries... The early silence in a telephone circuit gave an opportunity for listening to stray electric currents that cannot be easily had today. I used to spend hours at night in the laboratory listening to many strange noises in the telephone and speculating as to their causes.

Thomas Watson,
in his memoir
Exploring Life (1926)

I want to talk about how Canada could be a model for the first country in the post-industrial economy to be more a state in process than a nation-state.

If we reject the corporatist concept of government, with its inevitable inequities and its orthodoxy of the bottom-line, with its economics stuck in a solution-based acceptance of linear logic, with its elevation of computer-programs and virtual concepts over humane individual response, then we reject the blueprints of slash and burn, downsizing and dehumanizing. When we rejected constitutional initiatives, we spontaneously recognized that our society does not need to rigidly codify itself. If we begin to perceive our strengths in the history of communications, in debate and experimentation, in the resistance to violent resolutions and arbitrary systems, then we may say that Canada is light, unburdened by constitutional weight and records of viciousness, by a military culture or a state religion.

We may acknowledge that we follow an alternative current in electric city, the vision of an imaginative culture, urbane and amenable, that puts forward the best self through reverie and solitude. While sensing that complete agreement is unlikely, friction and contradiction our heritage, improvisation our past and present, compromise our hope, we have the opportunity to reassess the nature of the political economy. In that review, which could become a revelation, we may see that Canada is a place still emerging, non-linear, swerving away from the rule of empire, full of subjectivities, without one dominant curbing view.

I'm not idealizing Canada. On the contrary, I take greed, humiliation, selfishness, and egotism to be facts in our lives. I am not sure that these forces in ourselves, and in our institutions, can be fully legislated away. I confess to my own ambivalences about a country that I've often thought about leaving. Apathy, narrow-mindedness, timidity, inertia, repressiveness, and a smug censoriousness can afflict us. The list of negative attributes could go on. And I have met far too many people in Canada who slavishly emulate the business-is-everything vulgarities of corporate New Yorkers or Londoners: these are the new colonial postures of those who want to travel in the borderless, or valueless, empire of capital. Moreover, I hesitate to endorse or advocate any sort of nationalism whatsoever. Any obsession with ethnic or nationalist exclusivity must bring ignorance and arrogance, chauvinism and factional warfare. It is cultural cosmopolitanism that has always attracted me. And yet I am a product of this country. The muses sometimes transcend geography; but truly the individual himself cannot always do so. Over the years, I've reflected on Canada, on what holds me here, and on what keeps bringing me back to the hints of authenticity and light. I've slowly come to identify what I call the alternative current, an approach to governing and society, citizenship and justice, that is centred in culture, in wisdom, art, science, and communications.

What could Canada be?

A state in process where values may prevail over policies. A place that accepts pluralism and multiple perspectives to be the grounds of our society. Canada's erratic styles and forms, its elusiveness, even its invisibility, make it a light space. That rootlessness could be a form of liberty; the unhoused quality, the sense of being freed from tribal membership, can be an imaginative release. It is a place where political leaders who take constitutional crises to be terminal points in time then meet people who take them to be provisional, only sketches and traces and not blueprints and maps, another part in the communications stories. A state that values the questions that concern the qualities and characters of the good life above the money and power society and its impoverishments of the soul and mind. A country where there exists "Wheel within Wheel", so Blake wrote in his *Jerusalem*, which could ease or at least modify and thus balance the relentless devouring push of transnational corporatism. A state evolving, both quickly and cautiously, beyond structures of extremist revolutions and reactions, if only we'd allow that unusual exploration to continue. A place where there is something sensed, lingering, hovering on the cusp of articulation, moving out gradually, appearing in stages, unfolding from the silence and the shadows. Ways of responding and thinking eventually lead to ways of living. Canada may be a place whose history and culture speak of this incognito difference: to communicate with the world rather than to conquer it. A state whose lack of a single identity, its lack of homogeneity, may be its destiny.

I'll give examples of what I mean by the alternative current in Canada through my personal experience.

I travelled across the country for more than three years. A divorce sent me spinning. Familiar ground had dropped out from under me, and I was lost. I moved from Toronto to Banff, to Calgary, and then back to Banff, and months alone in the healing air of the mountains. I was living cheaply, thinking, writing, putting things together again. Later I went to Montreal and on to Quebec City at Christmas, New Year's, and the carnival time. I came back to Toronto and lived for awhile out of a suitcase, a displaced existence. Then my life changed when I met someone, felt love, the stirrings and yearnings of reconnection, and remarried. My wife and I travelled in Southern and Eastern Ontario, stopping in small towns and villages, beside rivers and lakes. We left Canada for a period, going to Key West, mile zero in North

America. When we came home, it was to Toronto, and a quiet neighbourhood.

In the midst of my restlessness, I found myself asking questions about Canada. I discovered variety everywhere. I saw no evidence of empire, nothing I could say was all-Canadian. Yet I sensed intangibles that said we are unique here.

In Banff, I talked to a Japanese businessman who was perplexed by the Meech Lake controversy. "Why try to unify a country so big, so radically different in every place I've visited?" he asked. "Why try to fix something that wasn't broken to begin with?"

When I visited Calgary, I met a business woman who said, "I do business by bickering." I asked her to explain what she meant. "Most of my clients live in Saskatchewan," she said. "And we're not supposed to get along. Local pride, you see. So we bicker, gripe, make snide comments, whine. Then we find something, make an agreement. And everyone invites the other over for dinner. We'd aired all our worries through complaint."

In Quebec City, I saw French-language magazines and tabloids that referred only to

Québécois concerns. I was struck by the passionate discussion of issues and personalities in the self-referential electronic media there. They spoke with conviction, love, and dissident anger. Their ties to their sense of place were profound, and I was moved by their emotional attachment. While I heard people ask, "Do *les anglais* truly hate us?" I did hear of pragmatic political affiliations and a long history, a tacit and understood connection with the rest of the country.

In Westport, Eastern Ontario, on the Rideau Canal System, I saw Victorian homes with hand-painted signs in windows that said, "Canada… Don't Give It Away…" I encountered people who muttered dark comments about how the government had sold out to Quebec. Yet in Westport harbour, I saw houseboats from Laval, Montreal, and Kingston moored at the overnight dock. And in the twilight, I heard people conversing in fractured combinations of English and French.

In downtown Toronto, I attended a biweekly discussion group, called the Committee for Debate, where entrepreneurs, consultants, politicians, and writers met to argue about political reform. Although the group disbanded—in a parody of the result of the constitutional conferences, no one could finally agree on anything—I heard the refrain: "How can we take power from the financial élites who don't have a feel for Canada?"

In Key West, I talked to vacationing Americans who were curious about their northern neighbour. "Is it true your country will break up and join the U.S.?" one asked. "Why would you want to do that?"

Back in Canada, I read pundits and editorialists in newspapers who staidly assured me that the country was plummeting towards dissolution. Then I read Salman Rushdie's words in *The Toronto Star* about how Canadians were moral leaders. "In the same way as the Nordic countries in Europe have a long track record in human rights," he said, "Canada is, so to speak, the Scandinavia of North America."

And in the classrooms where I teach, I heard students say that their country was elusive to them. They nevertheless said that they were immersed in a quality of life that differed from other countries, and they were adamant when they said that they didn't want to be anything other than Canadian.

Then late one night I stopped at a Tim Horton Donuts shop on Queen Street East, pausing on my way home from downtown, and

I heard night people, roughened men and women, muttering about feeling cut off, about feeling lonely, powerless. I sat down and listened, and I started jotting down fragments of what they said on a napkin.

"Government is leaving us out. Not part of what they think is okay. How can anyone get along like a corporation? Unions letting us down. Everyone letting go. Goddamned PM. Fuckin' difficult to hold onto a buck. Out for a job. Banging on doors. Hitting the pavement. Any luck today? No way. Gotta hang on. When you don't get what the fuck. Yeah livin' like my hand's out all the time. Passing us by. Wish I could get out. Someplace other than the streets. But hey they're my home y'know. Goddamned people know nothing. But I keep going out, getting out."

The shop was a badly lit midnight gathering place–a replacement for a refuge where there would be familiarity, recognition. And there were words, even in a spot where I sensed despair, words trying to shape sense, grasp at the truth. I felt far away from these people; yet I knew they too wanted to know what it means to be valued. How easy it would be to overlook these feelings of diminishment, of severing.

Through these meetings and talks and incidents and travels, I discerned a latent question about this anti-nation, its loose ties and hidden assumptions. We may have misunderstood the process we are experiencing, and we may have missed something that already flourishes here. By looking for constitutional guarantees and absolutes, and by allowing politicians to turn our national debate into a question about whether or not we can afford Canada, we may have lost the implicit need and willingness to explore, sample, examine and live truly, that which has made each part of the country unusual. We do not lack cohesion: this comes from dialogue and civility, the participation in differing views, our emergence through argument, counter-argument, airwaves, and mixed messages, the intangibles that we know through glimmers and clues. Canada is like several puzzles that we're all working on at the same time: everyone has a part to add but no one has seen a whole picture yet. So we must inevitably balance on the edge of bitter disappointment, close to collapse, close to failure. I found the country to be an intricate pattern with many centres, where the tensions between the individual and the collective continue in their bewildering, risky course. Revaluations, review: I sensed some readiness to open, to move through suffering, to exist both in solitude and in communities, to be willing to live a difference, to turn away from destructiveness and impoverishment (of the life, of the soul), toward something full-hearted, good beyond what we now perceive, because we have never allowed ourselves to become fully snared in any one concept or structure.

I turn to an incident I saw on Canada Day, July 1, 1992.

I lived then on a tree-lined street in north Toronto. The area was like a small town. My neighbours discussed politics in a good-natured, sceptical way. The future of the country clearly mattered to them. But during that spring and summer, economic gloom possessed people. And on TV, on the radio and in the newspapers, we were exposed to a constitutional debate that we knew would not be resolved; its bulky pre-scriptions and conclusions could not satisfy everyone.

Then I saw surprising sights. I'd go for a walk around the block, and I'd see the Canadian flag taped to windows, fluttering over doors. This was unusual. Unlike the Americans I know, with their ferocious, fanatical devotion to the Stars and Stripes, most of my neighbours have said they aren't sure if they like the stark red-and-white design with the maple leaf stuck in the middle. On that Canada Day, when I went out strolling, I saw flags, birthday cards attached to doors, and other signs and symbols.

Quietly, the neighbourhood began to express its pride and faith. No one asked them to do so. In spite of the politicians and their warnings about the end of the country, something deeply felt endured. I had the impression that the people on my street had recognized an essence that the rulers had overlooked, forgotten, or maybe never knew.

The soul of the country lives on in the value of debate and in the knowledge that the probing must continue.

I acknowledge a paradox in my argument about the alternative current in Canada: the Free Trade Agreement recognizes the fact of the planetary culture and economy.

The apologists for Free Trade say that its benefits will soon reveal themselves. What I confirm is that the open-border approach to economics was inevitable.

Raw data spews across borders in the global society. Strange noises scat at night. Through computer networks, transnationals can transfer their capital in one day from Chicago to London and Zurich, from Tokyo to New York City and Toronto. TV and computer screens raygun images and words and numbers in our offices and homes. Satellite dishes, radios, cellular telephones, and answering machines shoot-up static into our psyches. Private neighbourhoods are nodes in this meshing of communication technologies, each street becoming abruptly like a highway for the rush and glint of the readouts. Overtones and subliminals–almost inaudible and indistinct messages on the edge of consciousness—murmur in our ears and minds. Invisible forces swirl. Something streams past, ungraspable and yet omnipresent, yanking us from our roots. This dataflux injects contradictory opinions, instant advice, entrancing fantasies, nightmare scenes of murder and ruin, paradisal moments of love and community, past-life recollections, auguries of a Utopian future, government propaganda and corporate advertisements, fundamentalist gospelling and Cyberpunk manifestos of revolt.

Free Trade may be the first shape of an economic and political corroboration of the electronic soundscape.

The accelerated pace of change makes all of our lives seemingly revolutionary. Like data junkies, we can live with our inside out, our outside wired in. Concepts of nation, nature, mind, and identity, seem to be amorphous, provisional, undergoing redefinition, or electrocution.

> When nature is eventually seen as refusing to express itself in the accepted language, the crisis explodes with the kind of violence that results from a breach of confidence. At this stage, all

intellectual resources are concentrated
on the search for a new language.

Thus say Ilya Prigogine and Isabelle Stengers
in *Order Out of Chaos: Man's New Dialogue
with Nature.* They write of their search for a
comprehension of context, an awareness of the
environment that we almost entirely create, in
part perceive. The irony: what I seek to describe
here through language may be beyond the reach
of the printed word. Our culture may have
metamorphosed into pure image and sound,
pictogram and vibration. Cross-border transfers
of data exist without legislative fiat.

I acknowledge the paradox in my argument
about Free Trade because I'm critical of the way
our leaders and politicians have managed these
transforming world models. They haven't satis-
factorily answered the pressing questions, whom
will the state serve? who will be the best managers and facilitators of this racing change? what
values should we preserve and affirm when trade
barriers tumble down, individual perspective
fractures, political borderlines vanish? who will
serve to balance the corporatist interests and
agendas that appear and then disappear behind
the acronyms IMF, GATT, NAFTA, and the

WB (the World Bank)? If no one can control these forces, legislate them into compliant citizenship, then who will be willing to influence, offer guidance? Who will provide the checks and balances, the mutes and dampers on the noise and rush?

We live absorbed in a whirl of panic and disarray, troubled and roused by visions, nightmares, collapses, liberating possibilities, all that accompanies the hyper-transformations. We lack a language yet for the infinite connections and variations, the patterns that unravel and unfold. And so we step hesitantly, sometimes awkwardly, across abysses, unsure that there is any ground beneath us. Every day brings more challenges and upsets to whatever consistency and definition we may have known. Intimate with the rolling and unrolling effects of mass technology, the waves, we nevertheless do not always know how to identify or precisely describe how machines mimic us (through simulation), encourage us to long for signs of ancestry (uprooted, we hunt for traces of the past, vestiges of family history, precedents in history, revivals of tribal membership), exaggerate our foibles (we see people on TV and movie screens, in the press becoming grotesques, cartoons), and converge (corporations move to meld all aspects of communications, dissolving lines between private life and work). We mainline electricity, the force-fields of the universe, through TV, radio, microwaves, fax machines, cellulars, and computers, and like acute receivers we reel, over-loaded, battered, unbalanced, suggestible.

We move in a culture that requires ways of perceiving technological effects which will inte-grate all media. When we join TV and radio and the computer with the old non-electric print technologies of the book and the newspaper, we could learn to become adept at reading the pres-ence, and maybe the essence, of those we elevate and elect. Eyewitnesses, earwitnesses, playing the ensemble of instruments, using the moments we have to become seers. These inven-tions may not only extend our faculties into space and time, thus wrenching our minds and searing our senses, they may at the same time help to restore humanist perspective to the mass sheen and wail of the teleworld. Replay, freeze-frame, slow-motion, fast-forward, image enhancement, storage and retrieval, sound echoes and amplifications, sampling and editing could galvanize us into achieving insight about those who appear on the screens and speak to us from radio bands, persuading and directing us, making their pitches and uttering their beliefs, both masking themselves and showing themselves, attempting to lead us.

Allow me to imagine what the alternative current could mean for Canada. I'd like to dream about a new pattern that joins thinking and intuition, another way of working and perceiving, a changed understanding of the political process and the effects that politicians can have on the moods and actions of others.

What is Canada? It could be a place without aggressive nationalisms, xenophobia and inflexible ideologies, charged in the flux of electronic technologies. Canadians could be a people who recognize that our country is a state in process rather than a nation with one absolute goal. It could be a state where questioning, ambiguity, privacies, the responsibility both to ourselves and to others, the multicultural dialogue and shifting borderlines, are allowed to become habits of mind. Our resistance to too many efforts to impose meaning through constitutional fiat can be healthy.

The mistake for us is to see ruinous confusion in the chaos. I observed earlier that the

Wilson manifesto was a free-enterprising template for an economy that had always been an arrangement of public-and-private sector alliances. The corporatist agenda sought to reconfigure Canada into a stock-exchange commodity. I stressed that the corporate-government studied the direction of our wealth, and focussed on Canada's rating in the terminals and databanks of the transnational money markets. Many of the corporatist questions were good ones: how do we restructure the economy to best serve people? how do we effectively channel wealth? However, the concern for deficit reduction soon led to the monomania about numbers and percentages. The politicians accurately apprehended the social, financial, and moral turbulence in electric city; their answers were callous and unimaginative.

When Joanne Kelleher interviewed Tom Peters—of *In Search of Excellence* fame—in *Computerland* (March 8, 1993), she asked, "What should IBM do to fix itself?" Peters replied: "Prayer would be my strongest suggestion." His seemingly flippant answer is not far from the alchemist's maxim: examine yourself. Explore your own motives and methods of proceeding. Concentrate; recognize strands of connection. Each of us is an instrument. Find out what is the best and the worst in us; transmute and transcend those powers. Our imaginations and souls hold the key.

The corporatist blueprint posed questions about wasted wealth. These problems must be grappled with by those we elect to govern. But there must be paths we can take without eliminating jobs and provoking panic. If we shifted our thinking, our states of perception, to conceive of another model, with different cultural premises, then our attention could be drawn to inventive action.

Let us fully imagine what is here, now: the stateless state where politics is not driven by fanatics, factionalism, and violence, by strict ideology and dogmatism, where the traditional cultures of the world can and do exist together. There are many languages in Canada, not just the official two; there are many cultures, not a homogeneous one. The danger in this myriad-minded approach is lasting division and isolation for people. The Canadian pattern could splinter into fragments that will never cohere. The polyphony could flip into an aimless jumble, an oppressive babble. Improvisation could become a groping after main themes. The country's paradoxes could become irreconcilable polarities. Ethnic groups could circle around themselves, excluding others, accusing one another of violation, nursing old wounds. But if we recall the summoning and announcement of the new in the symbol of the CN Tower–a spire whose essential use is the reception and transmission of multiple messages–then we could hold on to the feel for this antenna society, the responsive and reflective zone of North American energies.

THIRD MEDITATION
A Canada of Light

Here is a sphere of change, change, change.
Through change consume change.

> From a transcription
> of ancient Sanskrit
> manuscripts

Quebec City, late February, 1991.

It was there that I began to think about a Canada of light, the enigma of the country, and how its variety and frictions could be its enduring qualities.

I lived briefly inside the city's walls. The Mulroney years were at their zenith; the government's financial and constitutional policies had become dramatically apparent. For the first time in my travels I did begin to wonder if Canada's federation would crack apart, to be eventually incorporated into a uniform North American economic block.

One morning, I walked along rue St-Denis, down to the Dufferin Terrace at the foot of the street. Cold air swept in off the frozen St. Lawrence. Blue sky and fresh snow from the evening before. The icy wind made the turrets, sooted spires, chimneys, and slanting roofs look sharp-edged in the white light. I saw the winding cobbled streets and antique buildings of *La Basse-Ville* to the south and the steel-sheeted business towers to the west.

Nowhere else in Canada could I see such an abrupt and beautiful contrast of the old world and the new. An image of harmony: there was the small scale of the town, lanes measured for walking and pausing; and the mirrorshade city, elevators and escalators rising and falling inside the towering corporate designs. The traditional structures, with their evocation of composure and slowness, balanced the trim, cool, rectilinear buildings and their impression of machines poised for high-speed escape from the earth's gravity.

And it came to me then that what politicians took to be cynicism was fear in people. The forces of fear had temporarily won in Canada. Anxiety was seeping inside everything, and everyone. How could you identify it? You could almost touch the worry, weariness, mistrust, and recoil in people's lives; fear and rage had become palpable. There was a closure in how we responded to news about the country's future.

What brought the fear? Where could you find one of its sources?

You could read it in systems of thought that used the language of downsizing and credit ratings. You could see it in the words that meant people would be sent whirling without a promise of relief, systems that meant wealth and privilege could be concentrated in the hands of the few, so that only the most ruthless would survive. The rulers weren't ignorant, incompetent people: they were bright-eyed zealots who were persuaded of their righteous mission. They spoke in the codes of the final answer, of enemies and exclusivity. In the often cryptic formulae that politicians uttered about restraint and help for the needy came the politics of elimination and polarization. Survival-of-the-Fittest capitalism was back. After a time of imaginative political exercise in the 1960s and early 1970s–furious times that often squandered financial resources–the opposing power had arisen in society and finally in government. This was the force of shutdowns and pink slips; it was the system of thought that said between the lines, "Canada doesn't really exist… We can't afford it, so let's make the best deal possible… Put aside your ideals… We know what's best for you… People want pragmatic politics… Uniqueness and originality must be sacrificed to the debt…"

I stood there on the terrace overlooking the river. Wind blew up snow drifts and white dunes.

Suddenly I realized that the forces of fear had hauled in their spiritual baggage of accusation and paranoia. The cold climate needed warm souls. But the mood in the country seemed to be rapidly becoming one where people shrugged off their rulers and mumbled, "That's only them doing things to us again… ramming things down our throats…"

The forces of fear had bought their victory with hardened hearts, deafened ears, blunted sensitivities, dimmed imaginations. In this numbness began irresponsibilities. Their success could only lead to a belief in will and necessity, in greed itself. And though I knew that will, necessity, rage, and even a portion of greed are essential to the growth of our souls, the three factors left out transcendent vision, philosophical foundation, culture and truth. They left out fairness and compassion, what we once called the good.

On the Dufferin Terrace, I looked back at the Chateau Frontenac, the small park, and the American Consulate, then I turned and gazed down at *La Basse-Ville*. I imagined something else then: my lost country. I knew how lost we were becoming while we made our journey into the cyclotrons of international finance and mobile currencies. I realized we were experiencing the loss of a frame of reference, a way of looking at colliding models of reality. We'd lost a tenor of life to which we'd grown accustomed. This led to frayed nerves, the whiplash of anger. Canada could be ripped apart by the hyperintensity of the telecommunication links. We suffered from a surfeit of interpretations and disconnected bits. The corporatist years in government had become a time of suspicion, near-hopelessness. Something had passed in Canada. I'd felt this passing in my life, and in my travels across the country.

Yet I thought that something could be found again in Canada, too. Even when I was away, I couldn't escape the feeling that a sounding of meaning, of purpose, was underway there. What was happening was pivotal, essential; a global story was finding crystalline drama. The mystery kept drawing me home.

I thought of Canada, of a time and place that seemingly had lost its way. Politicians and business leaders were in danger of becoming oblivious to this sense of loss. I'd observed the impact of overload in their conflicting opinions, the steeling of their positions. I saw how many people had lost direction in their lives. I'd witnessed how leaders of almost every party, in every government, were leaving a bequest of delusions about eliminating deficits (rather than managing them), a legacy that was solidifying into a stringent, absolutist approach to economics. It was becoming clear that economics ruled every decision, every angle. No other concern seemed to enter the minds of the rulers, and the result was the obsession with power only.

We'd become lost, and for some people the country no longer appeared to expand towards some Canada of light and air and wind, a big land open to welcoming spirits and fresh imaginings.

Where were we to start again?

If we were to be discoverers, we had to engage and reimagine our perceptions of the communication fields and their hyper-transformations. It was unlikely that anyone could escape the barrages and radical diffusions of data, the sensory simulations and the virtual simulations of the wired-in life. I knew there was a lot to learn about being hooked up; how an individual could be critical and absorbed, moved and detached, implicated and observant, pliant and rebellious. There was more to be learned, more to be said, I thought, about the secret country and its contradictory moods.

Later, when I returned to Toronto, I began to think about the meaning of a Canada of light. When I walked around the city, I reflected on its wild urban sprawl, and the ambitious architects of the high towers downtown. I sometimes carried books with me, works by Vaclav Havel and Blake. In Havel's essay, "Paradise Lost," I read this passage on the political process:

> Those who find themselves in politics therefore bear a heightened responsibility for the moral state of society, and it is their responsibility to seek out the best in that

society, to develop it and strength-
en it …

I saw the politicians in the corporatist mould
had spoken–often unconsciously–to the worst
in us. They'd addressed the drive for power, the
need to belong to larger protectorates and
systems; they had encouraged, again maybe
inadvertently, the extreme polarizations of
wealth, and had helped to dull and inhibit our
imaginative volition and reach.

I put Havel's lines together in my mind with
a statement I remembered from Robert Pirsig's
Zen and the Art of Motorcycle Maintenance.

If a revolution destroys a systematic government, but the systematic
patterns of thought that produced
that government are left intact,
then those patterns will repeat
themselves in the succeeding government.

Those thoughts illuminated for me the
cycles of entrapment and oppression that Blake
described in his prophetic epics and lyrics. I read

and understood his lines where he stated his visionary intention to break confining cycles, all limiting mechanisms of thought, and inspire us to become creator-citizens, who are

> Striving with Systems to deliver
> individuals
> from those Systems…

Look at your selves first, these poets and philosophers recommended and exhorted: know your souls, your values, your mind, what the world means to you, what you want the world to be. If you want to know how power moves, how ideology and assumptions and prejudices and plans, in fact tyranny itself, can move those who are in government and those who run the transnationals, then understand your own ambitions and needs, motives and actions. Like man, like state. To put this baldly: man is his state.

To break with the cycles of imposition and the effects of hard economic policies will take brave, inventive people. But Canada has always been an intangible and difficult place. We persist in perceiving the traces of the alternative current, the aspirations of a high humanism, another way of imagining our state and the relations and responsibilities between ourselves and governing, so that somewhere moral courage and dreaming, mediation and experimentation, will thrive.

An enlightened state would have to exist more lightly than a nation bloated by constitutional restrictions, the administrations of an empire, borderlines and colonies and protectorates to police with a military establishment and a National Security Council. Such a state would be an evolutionary civilization rather than a revolutionary society.

> ... real peace... must always rest upon a peace of mind; whereas the so-called armed peace, as it now exists in all countries, is the absence of peace of mind. One trusts neither oneself nor one's neighbours, and, half from hatred, half from fear, does not lay down arms. Rather perish than hate and fear, and twice rather perish than make oneself hated and feared–this

must some day become the highest maxim for every single com-
monwealth.

Unexpected words from Friedrich Nietzsche.
They are words which speak directly to a
country like Canada, founded mostly without
violence, preserved mostly without violence.

By a light state I do not mean a political and
social Utopia. Josef Skvorecky may write in *The
Engineer of Human Souls*, through the eyes of his
central character, Daniel Smiricky, that:

> The Toronto skyline is more beau-
> tiful to me than the familiar sil-
> houette of Prague Castle. There is
> beauty everywhere on earth, but
> there is greater beauty in those
> places where one feels that sense of
> age which comes from no longer
> having to put off one's dreams
> until some improbable future...

But every place and time has its furies, its
turmoil, its inequities, its horrors. Experimental
heavens launched through social engineering

have a habit of turning into hells. There is a
share of intolerance, brutality, stupidity, and
guilt in Canada—the treatment of aboriginals,
the battles of the Northwest Rebellion, the
Winnipeg riots on Bloody Saturday in June
1919, the internment of Japanese Canadians
during World War II, the War Measures Act in
1970—there is degradation for the homeless who
tramp the streets, a humiliating entrapment and
frustration for those who live under the poverty
line, unfairness and abuse in businesses, schools
and homes. No state must ever be an end in
itself. I do, however, sense the potential for
another kind of relationship here between citizen
and government, culture and communications,
the country and the world.

Moreover, I believe the possibility of Utopia
must exist for us. We feel its absence; we reflect
on the influence of its ideal; we dismiss it, fear
it, demonize it, call it unrealistic, call it unat-
tainable; yet we long for it: our every political,
social aspiration, all our yearnings for warmth
and kindness, recall it and conjure it. Any design
of a country that does not include at least the
possibility of Utopia is not a design worth
believing in or extolling.

So leave Canada to its lightness. Let us tell whomever comes to power to let the country be light, not weighted down by eighteenth-and-nineteenth century concepts of nationhood, theoretical grids and templates, the formal apparatus of a homogenizing economic system and legislation that attempt once and for all to resolve the disparate elements and paradoxes that make up this society. Leave it to its ambivalences, its frictions, its civility, its anonymity, its mystery, its slow unfolding; leave it to the debate, the haggling and wheedling and coaxing. Drop the need to find lasting solutions for what may not be a problem. Meaning may reside for us in the way that we address injustices, in the dialogues we support, in the messages we send, and in what we intuit about our secret selves.

A digital simulation in a computer works through a pattern of light, a pattern of shadows. One could make an imaginative leap: every person also reflects and emanates their own light

and shadow, a free-floating side to their personality and a tragic, murderous, power-hungry
dimension. We project our darkness and light
into the world. The Canadian shadow often
appears to us in the shape of the United States
and the constantly looming prospect of assimilation. We play in a pattern of light to their
burdened, darker history.

Whatever we allow to develop in Canada
should continue without warnings and threats
from politicians about an imminent national
Judgement Day. Then what grows here could
be rich, original, humane, quietly audacious,
full of eccentricities and discontinuities.
Evolution over revolution, metamorphosis over
Armageddon–these could be our credos. An
overly formulated and detailed constitution is a
recipe for madness. Let us sustain our native
irony for all things official, imposed, and uni-
tary. Rather than look for political unity–an
ultimately futile question and pursuit–let us
look for harmony, the deeper arrangement and
cohesiveness of conflicts. Let us welcome what
is multifarious, flexible, personalized, paradoxical, and protean.

What will connect us? What gives us vision and voice? I venture this: under the official news, the editorials and opinions, the corporatist propaganda and the prepared speeches of many rulers, and the soul's chatter which comes with the noise of our media daze, people sense a spirit and a motion, not yet articulated, still felt, one possessed by premonitions of hope and transformation. When a government or a transnational turns its citizens or workers into objects, digits, counters, and decimal points, then people may begin to feel acutely human in their estrangement. Alienation and loneliness plant the seeds for rebellion and consciousness, new stages of learning. What systems, polls, and corporate strategies deny is the aspiring individual, the source of purpose and value. Systems always push things downwards; their method is one which imposes structure, freezes meaning. It's the individual who must learn how to rise up, evaluate, interpret, and care. Paradoxically, the severe bottomline approach to the economy–programmed by people whose responsibility and compassion, awareness and generosity we question–may inspire the vital contrary move: the desire to retrieve personal authenticity, a humanism that may balance the images, spectres, glows, and bytes, the fantasias and ethereality of the electroscape we created but cannot control.

Politicians and business leaders have tapped into economic, electronic, social, psychological, and psychic energies that they don't understand. They did not foresee the effects of what they glibly called a deregulation, a revaluing of wealth.

The Russian philosopher and dissident, Alexander Herzen, in *From the Other Shore*, an essay he wrote more than one hundred years ago, said this about such engineering:

> If progress is the goal, for whom are we working? Who is this Moloch who, as the toilers approach him, instead of rewarding them, draws back... a goal which is infinitely remote is no

goal, only… a deception; a goal must be closer—at the very least the labourer's wage, or pleasure in work performed.

May each election and referendum continue to shake us to our roots. In those paroxysms—our civil replacements for wars and revolutions—we may find out what our country is made of and what values we want to hold.

Envision a place that preserves the capacity to respond, where sensibilities have not been stunted by too much power, comfort, conventional thinking, restlessness, or wealth, or by too little power, despair, inertia, desperation, or poverty, where minds haven't been thoroughly propagandized by a single theory or approach. Envision a country where the interior life, the life of imagination, of conscience, of sympathy and concern, can prosper in tacit, subtle resistance to commercial spectacle. I imagine a place that is fit for dreaming truly. Canada's *raison d'être* is a slower rhythm, sudden outbreaks called elections and referenda that incite and inspire insight, the discovery of links, and the permission to be frictive. Without a compelling case for cultural meaning, then everything becomes an economic arrangement, a soulless politics of deals. Envision a country; ours is here, still evolving.

We will need politicians who are more than mere handlers and facilitators of power and deals. We need anti-politicians, as it were, who can contemplate and advocate the profound ambiguities and ambivalences of our country. It's good for leaders to be constantly challenged; referenda and elections put leadership on notice. And what will citizens need? Patience and gentleness, the time to learn and disagree, to recognize the implicit pattern of contraries at play, the time to prepare to resist those who seek to encode rupture, leading us into a final estrangement both from each other and from the civilization we are building.

If we could see in the confusion and hear in the noise that new structures of consciousness are emerging, then we may say that the communication state we both create and inhabit could become our identity, our offering to the world.

If we could see that our light state may in fact be a condition of receptivity, of openness, of living without borderlines, of trust and the willingness to talk and to debate, then we may say that breakdown is part of the process, setback is a kind of gift, and we may then step back from apocalyptic gloom and cataclysmic finale, and the rapacities of consumption and greed. We may acknowledge that the nation-state is disappearing, and the new model is decentralized, metamorphic, mythic, planetary, complex.

If we could see that we can't stop the attractions and repulsions of electricity, that our technologies amplify the effects of electromagnetism on us, then we could see that we are moving into world embrace, a deeper and quicker witnessing of lives and events, of the range of human consciousness and behaviour.

If we could see that through multimedia convergence we are recognizing ourselves, engaging the human conundrum and situation, *existenz* itself, in incessant feedback, in ways that we could not have conceived decades ago (a circumstance resembling the first time people saw themselves in mirrors, not fully realizing how the reflecting glass can distort, exaggerate, reveal, and flatter, all while showing how you look from a reversed perspective), then we may say that some honed, awareness stirs, and that our lives are now inherently, radically visionary.

If we could see how electronic eyes and ears automatically confer clairvoyance and clairaudience on everyone who wears and uses the instruments available, then we may understand the exhilaration and terror that follow our visionary present.

If we could see that our state is built from variety, not uniformity, and that unity must be implicit and not explicit, then we may say that what we have is a tremendous space of light and air, with grounding in questions of justice.

If we could see that many people share the hunger for justice, for the human mind and sensorium to ponder and grasp what it means to have a life of quality, then the fear that accompanies *accelerando* technological change could be transformed into an influx of intuitions, thoughts, resources, and needs.

If our dreams can last, then we could turn our time and place to gold.

Why are we here?

To be something new, to make a difference, in the wilderness of power and pain, in the arenas of exploitation and humiliation. Only this process of engagement can exalt and exhilarate us. We may not be able to prevent suffering, or degradation—we may not be able to stop the insufferable arrogance and insensitivity of those who purport to lead and manage us—but we may be able to make all of this less the case. So we must be tough visionaries, keen and reasonable, daring tragedy, aware of our propensity for apathy, ignorance, avarice, and savagery. Then we may say that Canada's hidden destiny is to follow a path that diverges from egotism and violence, and to build a place where people could say, "All the forces and contradictions, the qualities and contrasts of our souls exist here side by side." Maybe then we will be able to wholly imagine the alternative current, perceive that we are evolving a state without walls, and comprehend how we are pioneering a society whose communications stories express the myths of receptivity and constant negotiation, the anonymous place, the many-sided state, the pluralistic country without a single identity. Then we may sense in the hints and static that we hear over the airwaves that Canada's very impossibility is its hope and its possibility.

CODA
A Prayer

May the ability to see many points of view
keep us gentle.

May the ability to see a future
keep us bold.

May the ability to recognize and reject
hardhearted iniquities and
needless cruelties keep us compassionate
and hopeful.

May the ability to perceive patterns that are
yet to be fully realized keep us clear
in our hearts and minds.

May the ability to communicate and
to face facts, and yet to dream new dreams and
to imagine fuller lives, give us the sweet
strength we need.